I REFUSE
TO BE

REV. LACY GREEN JR.

ISBN 978-1-0980-1518-3 (paperback)
ISBN 978-1-0980-1519-0 (digital)

Christian Faith Publishing, Inc.
832 Park Avenue
Meadville, PA 16335
www.christianfaithpublishing.com

Unless otherwise indicated, all scripture is quotation from the Holy Bible the Dake annotated Reference, King James Version Large Note Edition by Finis Jennings Dake. Copyright 1961, 1989 by Finis Jennings Dake

Printed in the United States of America

I dedicate this little book to my mother and father, my loving parents, Lacy Green Sr. and Evangelist Willina Smutherman Green, who struggled day and night raising us the right way. Leading us to the Lord early in life so we could truly understand the truth. I also dedicate the pages of this to my sisters and brothers who are the core of my heart, all my friends and neighbors, and my spiritual father Pastor Johnny O. Coe, who have made deposits into my life and to whom I esteem more highly than myself.

The late Rev. Glover, Rev. Davis, great friends and pastors. Who will always be within me as such. Rev. Larry Mc Callum, Mother Page, Mother Emma Mc Bride who cradled me when I was a child. Pastor E. Goings.

A lifelong friend, of course, Rev. Bishop Julius McAllister, former dean of the board of examiners AME, Florence, SC, and all of my friends and teachers there. Bishop O. T. Johnson, the late Pastor Hooper and Pastor Eddie Mayner.

Minister Don Cooper, Pastor Franklin Myers, all of my friends I've had the privilege to be ordained with, and the elders that I've had the joy of serving with. Rev. Thelma Mack, Rev. Eugene Dunson, Evangelist Letha Mae Bunkum, and then some new to the ministry: Rev. Glen McClellen and Rev. Eva Smith. And my new friend Pastor John Whittfield who is the watcher over my soul now. And honoring all my ministers, officers, saints, and friends of Love And Joy Christian Center.

These are just a few of the people I owe so much to. But most of all, this is to my wife, Emma Lee Taylor Green, who has stood by me through thick and thin. This journey with her has been amazing to me. Thank you all.

CONTENTS

ACKNOWLEDGMENTS

When God inspired me to write this book, I called on all my memories of the past, good and bad, happy and sad, because through it he would help somebody out there to maybe understand *that this journey* is for real and your purpose is for real. The calling of the royal priesthood is nay. I've had many special people in my life who have made so many deposits preparing me for what was ahead. They are so valuable to me because of the knowledge and wisdom they have shared during our conversations, our studies, and in our messages from the pulpit.

I am thankful to God for placing them in my life at the appropriate season, and for the harvest that his kingdom will birth forth. My friends, I love and cherish our journey together. May God's blessings now manifesting in your ministry continue, and all of your household prosper.

PREFACE

What is it that you refuse to be?

Jesus *is the author and finisher of our faith*. God has given every man the measure of faith, but to build it up, you must have events in your life that will allow the development of strength so the individual becomes stronger in the faith. Faith without works is dead, so you got to work your faith. Faith comes by hearing, and hearing the word of God over and over again and again until it permeates into your very spirit. Learn to call the things that are not as though they were. Use that godly kind of faith, and whatever you asks in Yeshuah's name will be yours. So refuse to be what you are not.

How is it that we as human beings have similar life experiences, but we make so many different choices. In the pages of this little book, I show some of the events that happened in my journey thus far and how *my decisions* were affected by *situations* and where I was in the Lord at the time. Sometimes out of position to be blessed. Sometimes out of God's will, and sometimes without the proper direction.

Refuse to be, as the evil one is! Realize that he is real, and Jesus is the way, the truth, and the life. The only begotten of the Father God Almighty. Who came that we may have life and have it more abundantly. Refuse to be as hardheaded as I was seeking fame and fortune when I needed only to seek the kingdom of God, for everything else would have been added as it has been now.

Can a man make his way back from a road of destruction? Can he change his mind, his life, his direction?

Join me through the pages of this book. You will laugh, cry, be strengthened and ready to return to the battlefield.

1

A LOSER

Hello, my friends, I would like to give you a greeting in the name of our Lord and Savior Jesus Christ, the Son of the Most High God, in whom we have the right to say Abba, Father and Father of all creation. I hope that the pages you are about to read give you an empowerment, a revelation, insight, relief, a breakthrough and increase you in your laughter and moral fiber. *There is a shifting in the atmosphere, and the power and will of God is manifesting itself right now.*

He is the very fiber of my being and the essence of my soul. I know Him. He is my all in all. For when I didn't know who I was, He cared for me until the appointed time. Now I know that Yawha, Ya-havah is God! Some say Jehovah, but since I've found out that in the Hebrew manuscripts and alphabets there is no letter *J*, I've decided to call Father by His proper name. And El-shidai, the many-breasted One, the God of more than enough, fills me and anoints me and meets all my needs according to his riches in glory.

Now it's time to change shoes for a while; you will walk in mine, and I'll walk in yours to see how well they fit. In changing shoes in this manner, I don't suspect that either of us will get athlete's foot. Even though all of our lives are connected in some way, the ways that we think and the environment in which we live in have a lot to do with how similar our life experiences are *or how different they can be.* An experience is just an experience until you tell somebody, then it becomes a testimony. Our paths are intertwined so that we follow the paths in which God has laid out for the chosen ones. Though all of us are His children, only a few will strive to be*come* His sons because all don't follow the intricate design of His plan for our lives.

All are heading in different directions until we start following the true one only. You have to wake up and see which way or plan that is. In this maturity *is* perfection, and vanity, such as wasting time, folly of life, and foolishness, have less of a chance to thrive and gain control of you.

No doubt, many of us growing up heard words or comment directed toward us, *our race, nationality, or religion,* that were of a *derogatory* or negative nature, and the intent was to assassinate our person or character depending on how we interpret what was said. If we would have believed these words, our heart's desires would have been hindered or delayed, and our growth or walk in life would have been dwarfed, be made a midget, or would have been made ineffective because of their belittling effect. Words do hurt; they have power, but none like the word of God. Life and death are in the power of the tongue. From the tongue comes curses and blessings, so we must always watch what we say to others as well as what we may say to ourselves. And as we know, it is so easy to lie to ourselves.

But there is something about becoming a child of God, a new creation that helps you change your way of thinking and acting. You don't talk like you used to talk, walk like you used to walk, or do what you used to do or at least that's how it's supposed to work. However, it takes a little time. That's called the transitioning period, which is the time involved with transforming your mind to think as Jesus thought. As the scripture reads, "Be ye not conformed to this world, but be ye transformed by the renewing of your mind." Before this, associates that we knew would say things about us, and we would get mad or angry, but now it's different or should be. Even though we may have heard it through the grapevine, gossip, or some other messenger, it should have held no merit if it didn't come from the true vine or if God didn't say it. We realize now that there are only two things this type of communication can do, and they are to encourage us or discourage us. Subconsciously, we take in things that hide in our subliminal thought patterns ready to show up in future times to paralyze us, poison us, or stagnate us. Hindering us in our process toward destiny. There are certain paths that God has laid out for each of us, and if we allow Satan to pull us away from that which is inevitable, pull us away from our source. Off our path, we are then out of position and maybe even out of His will to receive His blessings, favor, grace, or mercy.

During the early years of my life when I was growing up in South Carolina, there were many of us who worked the fields to earn money to feed and support our families. There was a lot of hatred and segregation, which sparked harsh words that were focused toward black and white people alike. The KKK was active, and terror filled the air because of racial tensions. Not that the KKK just hated African Americans 'cause I think they hated everybody who was not white. And then the poor whites were no account to them. The things that I heard when I was a little boy would not have motivated me to be anything else but less desirable. Name-calling, fights, picking, prejudice, lynching, and all types of mess that disturbed my soul.

The fight for civil rights had not yet been won, and people of different races had fear of one another. But my earthly father had a spirit of excellence locked up in him, and he saw a better way. A greater vision that led us down the road toward a reachable goal to allow his eight children a chance to be more than a suppressed people or a menace to society. For some are held in bondage to where they came from, who their parents were, what race they are, whether they were poor or well-to-do, or did or didn't have. A change had to be made in our lives to enable us to carry on and survive mentally, spiritually, and physically. For we had to be delivered from the brainwashing we suffered as the servant class where many were slaves to what others thought of them. Racial barriers were placed in front of us to hinder our development, and stumbling blocks were placed in our way to give some hate monger a reason to burn down a church, burn a cross in your yard or house, or worse. This in itself was enough to slow progress because of fears that was as real as hellfire to the unrepentant sinner.

We had to struggle many times to get our next meal, but no matter what new challenges were brought forth, this change had to be made. Stagnation is not salvation; overcoming suppressions is, and in that is deliverance. And we are overcomers. Sometimes you have to fight for a chance! And we were surrounded by friends and neighbors who had our back. We would help each other back then, and if they had it, you had it.

Our family moved from the farm that we were living on to a house about five miles away. My father landed a job at the textile plant by the name of Dixieanna Mills where they produced carpet for a company by the name of Mohasco. A far cry from the environment of farming tobacco, cotton, cucumbers, so forth and so on, I know and even thought we as children still did this type of work. As hired hands, we received more for our labor than we did while sharecropping, and this assisted in supporting the family.

There was an increase in our household, but also there was an increase in the cost of living, and there were many areas where we still went lacking. But can I tell you something that is very funny? Buckle your seat belts 'cause you're gonna love this! We were free! And it felt so good just to be in a better place in life.

Many days we went to school carrying our lunch in a grease-covered brown bag, wearing hand-me-downs and patches on the rags that we covered our loins with. We received them from families that had no further need of them. I mean many of the kids got new clothes for the new school year; we got new rags. We got stuff such as socks with holes in them where your pinky toe was supposed to be. I found myself wearing little girl's underwear; however, I was only between six and nine years old. Mind you. I didn't know any difference. That was until an older boy at school told me, "Aye, you got on girl draws!" As you know, this got around school pretty fast. "Aye, he's wearing girl drawers!" He told everybody. Have you ever been around people who will run stuff in the ground like this? I just want to know. His bucket had a hole in it. Poor fellow couldn't hold water. I've learned that a blessing is a blessing, and beggars can't be choosy, and a big-mouth usually gets a fist stuck in it. *Opps, oh I'm sorry. God's still working on me.*

We always listened to our mother telling us that God just keeps on making a way out of no way, and we thanked Him for all things 'cause He kept on blessing us. But we were being picked on every day because of the way we looked, what we wore, or what we ate. As I look at it now, I can see some humor in it, but then it left a bitter taste in my mouth. I still have problems when I see other children picking on someone less fortunate, and how it toxifies them even to the point of hatred. Schools and other things had not yet been integrated, and we didn't understand how the upper class lived. They had new books, new desks, a mind-set of success while we were still trying to figure out how to get a life.

Now I know that it was necessary to make us stronger, for if you cut a butterfly out of his cocoon, he would die because there were no obstacles there that he could press against to develop his muscles. So flying would be impossible. Sometimes a baby has to leave it's comfort zone to grow up. It has to keep falling until it can stand on its own two feet. So if you want to soar like the eagle, you have to develop strong-enough wings to carry you and learn how to fly against the wind. So be strong. Don't give up to easily!

However, many days went by where we had to fight because of people taunting us, pushing us around, calling us out of our name, and being aggravated already, they added more fuel to the fire by saying derogatory things about a couple that were doing all they could to raise their kids right: my mother and father. I never did care about "yo mama or yo daddy" jokes. That stuff made you want to hurt somebody! Ha ha, *I'm not a violent person—but never ran from a confrontation, even when the odds were against me.*

The greatest lesson I ever learned was when I took a licking for my sister Helen. My name could have been Timex 'cause I took a lot of beatings, but I kept on ticking; however, in this particular one, it was in defense of my sister. This young man I was about to exchange blows with was bigger than I was and older than I. His arms were longer, and he was schooled well on how to box by his older brothers. I had nobody that could teach me. I was the oldest child, so I had to literally learn from the school of hard knocks. After he pushed my sister down, I raced over to pick her up. 'Cause won't nobody gonna hit my sister and get away with it but me!

Seeing her little dress dirty after she tried so hard all day to keep it clean made my blood boil. I balled up my fist, filled my cheeks with air, struck out my chest, and paused a second, and nothing probably would have happened. I just had to show my teeth. But seeing him laugh about what he had just done sent a rage through me that felt like the fire of the Holy Ghost. Then looking back at Helen crying let me know I had to do something. The better thing to do would have been to walk away, but that didn't happen.

You see, she looked up to me to keep people from hurting her. My sister's nickname was Beanie Beanie. I always thought it was cute, but I called her by her true name, Helen Irene Green. One out of four beautiful sisters God blessed me with, and I was her hero. And that's how we find ourselves looking up to God, saying, "Father! Don't let them hurt me," and I put myself in God's place. And I stepped to the boy, but before I got in arms reach, He punched me in the nose and then he hit me in my eye. And I then realized that I wasn't God! 'Cause God doesn't bleed. I felt something dripping down my face, and at that moment, I had a revelation that let me know that this wasn't gonna be as easy as I thought it was gonna be. I mean before you get in a fight, you feel that you are invincible, headstrong as if you can beat anyone, and then reality hits, and I mean that literally. After the adrenaline wears off and you lose your toughman high, you're on your own. My anger had done, set me up for the knock-down, and I got fear in me.

The kids were yelling. Some for me, and some for him, saying, "Get 'em, Lace!" Then the other side, said, "Hit 'em again, Paul!" And Paul was giving it all he had.

He continued to hit me, and every time he hit me, his fist got redder with my blood. Drip, drip, drippity drop. I was stuck between a rock and a hard place, and I couldn't see no way out. This thing was not gonna end early. I mean Paul; he was having too much fun (the time of his life). Very seldom do you get to beat up two people in the same day, *in the same family*! Boy! He was building up a great reputation. I grabbed Paul and dragged him to the ground. But somehow, he managed to get on top and started punching away at me again. Today, I believe, they call that move "the ground and pound"!

You could just hear the thoughts of the meek and passive kids that ran away from situations like this one, saying, *Wow*! I'm glad that ain't me! See, Paul was one of the school bullies, and he got a lot of practice beating kids up. The kids were so scared of him that it very seldomly got reported. I can still name all of the bullies that were in our school. But Paul had been held back in school for two years, so he wasn't happy about that either. Could be the reason why he was whooping up on me something terrible, like he was taking his end of the year test, and he was passing. I give him an A+ for effort myself 'cause he didn't miss a stroke baby. If I were on the outside looking in, I probably would have enjoyed this fight myself. Suddenly!

Something on the inside of me cried, "God! Make him stop!" Then I heard a voice shout as someone was coming up behind me, saying "*Stop*!!! Don't you hit him no more!" And I, being half-dazed, said to myself, "You tell 'em God!" When I saw who it was, even though I was bleeding everywhere, I felt no pain 'cause the feeling in my face had better sense than I did, and it left a minute ago. It was my friend Michael who lived across the road from us. Then Mike pulled Paul off me and came around and stood directly in front of me facing the boy and said, "Before you hit him again, you're gonna have to go through me!" I looked around Mike then put on my best mad face 'cause I knew that Paul didn't want no part of that. Then Paul stood back and shouted, "He lost anyway, he ain't nothing but a loser!" Then before Mike really got on him, he made a quick exit stage, left, and Mike said, "Don't pay him no mind, Lacy Boy!" That's what they used to call me 'cause my dad's name was Lacy too. I guess that was better than being called Junior. That's what they called my cousin.

Then Mike said something that made me feel better. He said, "Paul is bigger than you and older than you, Lace. He ain't nothing but a bully. No way nobody else would have tried to fight him." And by that time, the feeling was coming back to my face, but this time with a vengeance. Inside my head felt it, felt like firecrackers were going off, and I thought to myself, *I believe they maybe a little smarter than me. 'Cause they run when they see Paul's around.*

That was my first real fight, but I know now that in order to be called a fight, both people need to be throwing punches. No, that wasn't a fight. That was a massacre. My first beating by another other than my mother. However, I've learned many things from this encounter. And they are:

1. People bigger than you tend to hit harder than you and usually have longer arms than you. But the other things I learned are good too!
2. Love will make you stand up to a seemingly unbeatable foe, but if you do your best against them, God will step in and fight your battle.
3. There is always somebody who looks up to you, no matter how insignificant you may think you are.
4. Many times you will have to stand against giants and evil-doers. But fear not, for he is with you, even until the end of this world.
5. Sometimes it's better to get knocked down than to lay down. Remember, God has your back, and if you can look up, you can get up.
6. Losing a little blood may hurt, but it doesn't make you a loser. Our Savior was crucified, bleeding on the cross, and he is still a winner and even to this day *be*cause of what He did, being covered in his blood still saves our soul.

And this one's very important:

7. Every fight you're in, you should learn from it, set up a strategy, and you will see ways that you can win if you don't quit! The adversary is always there; don't drop your guard. God wrote us a letter to teach us how to fight him!

Like I learned a guy with longer arms has a tendency to be able to hit you first! Ha ha, however, if you know how to duck, how to cover up, and roll with the punches. His weapons are less effective. If you know how to block, you can counter his attack; if you know how to defend, you can nullify his aggressiveness.

And if you know when to attack, he will have to change his strategy because he's gonna be getting hit as much as you or more, and people who are used to dishing out punishment aren't very good at taking it. This puts up a resistance. Resist the devil, and he will flee. He doesn't like to work hard anyway. A hard target is not easy prey.

That's how the devil is: he likes to hit you before you know what's coming, catch you by surprise so that you have no defense. But if you learn how to roll with the punches (that is, go through keeping the faith and walking in the word) no weapon that is formed against you shall prosper. No, my friend. Losing a fight doesn't make you a loser, but never willing to fight might. In the book of Psalms 144, David asked God to teach them to war so they could defeat their enemies because taking the territory called for much warfare. And we got to take back what the devil stole from us. The verse reads, "Blessed is the Lord my strength, which teacheth my hands to war, and my fingers to fight."

And I have learned that in this life, many battles will be fought. Many possibilities directed toward you, and you have to be a warrior. Remember the scriptures. I can do all things through Christ who strengthens me, and as long as He strengthens me, I am a spiritual superman, and the blood that covers me acts as lead to the devil's kryptonite. It has no effect.

A lot of the things you've been through were God's way to help you grow stronger for His purpose, preparing you for a time such as this. And as Paul the apostle of Christ said in one of his great epistles, "When I was a child I thought as a child I acted as a child, but when I became a man, I put away childish things."

This doesn't mean that we stop fighting for what we believe is right. Just make sure that it coincides with the will and word of God, and we change our method of combat, for now we really know who our enemy is. By refusing to be a loser, we resist what the enemy wants us to think about ourselves, for it's contrary to what the word of God says: we are as spirit-born believers. Born from above and filled with His Holy Spirit. Now I *know who I really am!* A son of the *most high!* I'm not afraid to do combat, whether physical or spiritual.

For He says that "I am the head and not the tail, above and not beneath, a lender and not a borrower, more than just a conqueror and at the end of this journey, at the end of this race, I win for victory is mine, and the reward is magnificent." I don't mean to preach, but you know it's a funny thing. The preacher in me always compliments: the God in me.

No matter how many times I get knocked down, I win. No matter how many bloody noses I get, I win. I have the will to get back up because I've been conditioned for this war, and I refuse to stay down because that feels worse than getting hit again. So I continue to press toward the mark of the higher calling which is in Christ Jesus, for I know that I am a winner and I refuse to be *a loser!* For my redeemer lives, and He lives in me!

2

WITHOUT DIRECTION

You know it's a funny thing to be able to see that you're missing something that is very important for your life.

You know, I have to tell you a story about a lost sheep that was trying to be its own shepherd. Somebody who tried to walk his own path instead of letting God direct his path. No, I'm not talking about Mary who had a little lamb. But it happened mainly because of ignorance, not of disobedience. And that person or lost sheep was little *ole* me. Now I know that ignorance is not an excuse, and disobedience is just that. Any way you look at it. We have a rebellious nature because of our flesh, and being hardheaded like a billy goat, we buck against things we don't care for or don't understand.

God Was My Protection

Being from a family that had two good parents, a mother and a father, *I've* had someone who had love enough to guide me always. Sometimes that meant tanning my rear end, but I turned out all right. My mother and father never spared the rod, and this let me know that they loved me. Even though it didn't fell to good, it kept us from running amok. However, it didn't keep me from going down the wrong road a time or two. No, I'm not *innocent* because they taught me right from wrong. After you know how to act, you then have to take responsibility for your actions. Sometimes you flirt with the devil to see if you will be a winner, and then you still lose: that's gambling.

However, I'm not talking about the point of being incarcerated or anything so awful; God shielded me from that. But I realize that there are many children at risk that don't have the supervision *and don't have this testimony*, the care or the love that would curve bad decisions possibly made by underprivileged individuals. Though a lot of the leadership we've received as children were not of a godly nature, it kept many of us within the boundaries of the laws of the land or it showed us how to get out of being caught. Many of us made it to this point without jail time, not because we were so good but because God was so good *to us;* and for that only reason, some of us are still free and still alive today. Because we didn't get caught and we didn't get caught up. See, God covered our tracks. He hid us from the enemy by placing his hedges around us 'cause even though we were told what would happen if we did a certain thing, we didn't know any better. But all have sinned and came short of the glory of God, but He didn't turn us over to the devil. Like always, somebody was praying for us little snotty nose children.

I can remember walking down that dusty clay dirt road from our house to St. Matthews AME Church, which was about four miles from us. My grandmother, whose name was Arletha, or as I used to call her Yesa, who was my father's mother, was a great part of our lives, and she made sure we got there. She was as sweet as a honeycomb. My father was her only child, and she took a lot of pleasure helping in the raising of us kids. My mother's mom's name is Martha, and she is a great grandmother too.

LOSING MY GRANDMOTHER

I can remember when I was about fourteen years of age, and that was the first time that death hit so close to home. My heart stopped 'cause Yesa called us to the hospital before she left us, and she said everything was all right, and a few days later, she was gone. It took me some time to figure out what she meant by all right, but I know now. She was saying I got my business fixed. That was the first time the world stood still for me; however, in the reality that we live in, life itself has to go on. For we have to take care of business until He comes.

Father was blessed after a little while to have us a brand-new house built with indoor plumbing, carpeted floors, lights in every room, no holes in the ceiling, no cracks in the walls, and even a garage to put the car in when we had a car. Boy, even our car had a house. We had really arrived in the Promised Land, but you got to understand where we had just come from.

We were living in a house with no running water. I had never lived in a house with running water before. I was now fourteen years of age. I didn't know any other way to live but hard. All the water we used had to be carried from my cousin's house because not even the pump would work.

Somebody to Wash Your Back

The closest thing we had to a shower was when it rained and the water came through the holes that nails left in the roof. *They were some bad carpenters*. When we took a bath, we had two methods. Either bath in the little tin tub or the big tin tub. We had to keep heating water so each child would be comfortable, but often it cooled before we finished. If you were one of the small kids, you did a twofer. That means two at a time, and there were eight of us. Four girls and four boys.

However, this was not all bad; I mean, at least we had someone near to wash our back. All I *have to say is* "Thank God for making a way out of no way."

We used an outhouse for a restroom, you know with the moon cut in the doors, like the Beverly Hillbillies before they moved to the mansion! That's where we did number two; we just did number one anywhere.

The area where we moved to was near Dillon, South Carolina, called Riverdale on a road named Pee Dee Church Road. The house still stands there today in excellent condition. My sister Letha still lives there near my sister Alice who's just down the road. She has a road named after her now. Alice Drive.

Alice is very talented. As a matter of fact, she is an outstanding playwright.

MEETING OUR NEW FRIENDS

After a while, the community started to develop quickly. There were only about two other homes in the settlement at this time, and the occupants were us, the Greens, the Blues, and the *Mcdowells*. This was the first time that we ever lived so close to people. These were our neighbors. As more houses were being built, and a dimly lit area became a brightly lit area, many families moved in. The McClouds, Coopers, Campbells, Freemans, Hamers, Floyds, and so on. All were great friends, but I believe the most memorable were the Ellis's because they had kids a little older than the other families.

There were two boys and two girls. The boys' names were James, whom we called bug. He was named after his father, and Johnny whose nickname was Boonzey, who was like a little brother to me. He was about one year younger, and two beautiful girls, Helen the oldest of them, and Cynthia who was the youngest. Their father's name was Mr. James, and we called him Mister Smitty, and I thought my dad was built, but Mister Smitty looked like Arnold Schwarzenegger, with rippling muscles everywhere. He worked on the railroad, and I believe that kept him in shape.

LETHA AND THE BOXING MATCH

Now we come to the mother whose name was Mrs. Bernice. She became my mother's best friend and the main instrument used in her salvation. She was a great part of our lives. The whole community loved her; she was a peacemaker when we kids had a fight. I remember once my little sister Letha was being picked on by some of the girls in the neighborhood. They wanted to fight her, but Mrs. Bernice asked them, "So y'all really want to fight her, huh?! I'll tell you what, I got some boxing gloves in the house if you want to duke it out?" Everyone shouted "yea!" So she put the gloves on one of the girls and my sister Letha, and it was on. Letha hit the girl who was bigger than her three times before she could say *ouch*. I was a little worried about her getting hit, but she proved to be tougher than I thought. Letha beat that girl like she stole something so fast, she was bug-eyed, stumbling over her feet because she didn't believe what was happening, waving her hands in the air, yelling, "I don't want to fight, no more! Take these things off me!" After that, Mrs. Bernice said, "Who's next?" But she couldn't run those girls down to put on any boxing gloves. She kept us all in church, and because their church, New Zion Holiness Church in Floyd Dale, South Carolina. was far from boring.

CHURCH FOLK: PHYSICAL EXERCISE PROFITS A LITTLE

They had a Christian band known as The Spiritual Echoes singing in the sanctuary. They used drums, guitars, cymbals, and keyboards. Boy, could they make a happy noise. We got so much exercise in church with jumping up and sitting down, when we got home it was time to lie down, but some didn't wait to get home. Some were slain in the spirit, but my natural mind back then thought that they were resting, just taking a nap because they covered them up with sheets and everything! It was like you couldn't sit down; you sit down and someone said, "Please stand for the reading of the Word." Then "Please stand for prayer." Then "please stand for the offering," and when the preacher was preaching, he would shout, "If anybody here loves the *Lawd!* You need to stand up on your feet, praise his name, and shout *hallelujah!*" I thought, *Why do we have all of these seats if we ain't gonna sit in 'em?*

Now Bug was our town clown and could make us laugh at the drop of a hat, especially when he would imitate church folk. You know a lot of people imitate church folks, and they talk about when you mess up to. So you could always say we went to church, but being children or teenagers, our minds weren't always on Jesus. However, she, Mrs. Bernice, was wise enough to know that if we were in church, we weren't somewhere breaking windows out of cars or breaking the law or setting your neighbor's houses on fire or on the street corners where nothing good was going on, but getting in trouble with the pusherman or police.

TURN-ONS ARE HARD TO TURN OFF

Bug was our educator or should I say our corrupter, and you know it was funny because he turned us on to girls, playing pool, cars, skipping school, fighting. Okay, that's enough about the turn-*ons*. The funny part is when you turn 'em on, it's hard to turn 'em off. It's called peer pressure, and our nature feels good doing things that appetize it. Being dared to do a thing just to fit in just felt right because of our carnal way of thinking. We called it being a part of a unit or click. We call it today *your homies* or a gang. That's a challenge that our flesh loves, for it gives us a reason to see what all we can get away with. But we stayed in the church, and many times we found ourselves going to the altar repenting for our sins not willingly, believe me, but only because our mothers found out about some of them.

We used to ask the elders "how do you know it's sin?" Now they took a shortcut when answering and told us, "If it felt good when you did it, it's sin." But we know now that if we do anything contrary to the word of God, we sin. Any shortcoming, anything against his commandments. But what was worse than that was the whipping we get now and at the end if we don't repent from the sin. I can remember our mothers standing up in the church, saying, "Some of you out there fell short this week. You sin, and you need to come to the altar." We waited until all the others got there and looked around at each other. Then in a louder voice, our mother's shouted, "Everybody who sinned, and you know who you are!" Not only did they know who we were, but they knew what we did too most of the time.

Always the Last to Come

But we were always the last ones to come. Our click numbered about eight. Bug, whose name was James; Boonzey, whose name was Johnny; Larry, whose name was James; Mitchell, Billy, Charles, Robert, and of course me, Lacy G. We would stay at that altar until our knees ached, and if we got up to soon, one of the mothers would push us back down and continue to pray over us. It was like the hands of God were on our shoulders, and we knew that wherever we were, we had eyes watching us.

First Shock at Christmas

But Bug was our leader. Bug was the first one to tell us that there was no Santa Claus. I didn't believe him. I kept on saying, "No, man, I saw Sandy Clause at the parade, and he came to our house one time driving a truck." I was about fifteen years old when I found out for real. I guess Mom and Dad didn't tell us 'cause they knew we would have spilled the beans for the smaller brothers and sisters. If my memory serves me correctly, I and Helen found out at the same time, the same year. What a bomb! I can remember like it was yesterday 'cause I didn't believe Bug. No, sir! Mom called me and said, "Lacy, come and get this cat out of the loaf for me before he tears up the insulation!" Dad was there to help me peak up into the loaf to get the cat. As I pushed the cover back, and I eased my head up in the hole, I saw all of the Christmas that they had brought for us. Mom asked, "Do you see the cat?"

I said, "No, ma'am."

Then she said, "What?"

Then I said, "Yes, ma'am!"

Then she said, "Here, take that bag and put him in it 'cause the kids are down here." And as they let me down, Mom looked at me and laughed and said, "Don't let the cat out of the bag now." And now since I got you in a place where you're already laughing at me, my legs wouldn't move 'cause I was in a whole heap a shock coming down out of that loaf. Felt like I was in the twilight zone. Can I trust you?

BIG GAME HUNTING

I'm gonna tell you something very funny. Can you keep a secret? Don't tell nobody else, okay? There was this little swimming pool not too far from the house where we guys used to go and skinny-dip. You know that when you got butt naked and swam. Bug found it. As a matter of fact, Bug found a lot of the trouble we got in. I loved him. Kept something going on. As a matter of fact, I can remember a wild boar hog that Bug found for us to hunt. Funny thing is that hog ended up hunting us and ran us up some trees with our little .22 riffle and all. But that's another story.

DINGLING, DINGLING

We had been warned by our parents not to go to that old sinkhole again, but we didn't listen, and we were just splashing around having a good ole time when our mother drove up in a car like Batman! In a flash, all you could see was little black booties *jingling and dinglings,* jumping up, climbing out of the backside of that hole, and running across the field and through the woods. I had all my little brothers with me. Kenny, Wayne, and Keith my baby brother. "Come back here, you boys!" They shouted. Knowing that we weren't going far 'cause we had just left our clothing. Boy, this was gonna be bad. Not only were we caught red-handed; we were caught bare-assed, and they weren't gonna let us put our clothes on until we paid them for our disobedience, with an open can of whoop ass.

LOOKING BAD FOR THE HOME TEAM

They stood at the car waving their belts and swishes as we covered our exposed backsides and everything else that we thought were personal. We could see them laughing at us behind their stern faces inside, saying with a giggle in their voices, "You shoulda thought about keeping them little things hid before you disobeyed us." Boy, did we still get our butts whipped, and as we walked home ashamed and sniffling, seemed as if the whole neighborhood knew about what just happened. But let me cut from this and take you to another time.

HOLY GHOST IN THE TENT

I remember it like it was yesterday. We used to have these old-time camp revivals and tent revivals that men of God like Bishop Charles Young, Bishop Barber, Dr. Jim Whittington, Oral Roberts, and more used to have. Not counting our community prophets like Mother Page, Evangelist Emma, and so on. But they would come and preach the hell out of us. There is this one time when I was about seventeen years old. Dr. Jim Whittington was the revivalist that week. Even me a sinner recognized a strangeness in the atmosphere which I knew was the Shikina Glory or the anointing of God's presence. It was very powerful, and he called me up out of about two hundred people, and I was near the back with Bug and the rest of the gang. I thought to myself, *Uh-oh.* God must have told him I done something. 'Cause you see even then I knew that God wasn't nothing to be played with. This is where my testimony began. He took my hands and gave me a word, saying you will be a great man of God, an exceptional preacher, a pastor of his flock, a prophet and warrior for His kingdom. I had no idea at the time what had just happened. What was this man talking about?

The wind was blowing and that tent we were under was vibrating. Made me say whoa. Going to church had not yet become a spiritual thing, but I was still religious and practiced, as most people do, the tradition of the type. Having the look of godliness but denying

29

the power thereof to me, I didn't know how to have a relationship with God. Of course, the fellows saw all of this happening, and when we got together afterward, they asked me, "What was he talking about, what did he tell you?" And I said, not being able to interpret what he, the man of God was saying, "He said I was gonna be a preacher. I don't know how to preach!" Anyway, I sin too much. The fellows they just giggled and said, "Yea, we know what you mean."

Back then, as I said, everything you did, if you were enjoying it, must have been a sin. But all that I was hearing in those days were seeds that would sprout up later in my life, for my whole life is a testimony, a book written by the hands of God for the path that he had set before me. I searched for the truth. I read the Old and New Testament of our Lord many times, but because I was still in the carnal state of nature, what we call the sinful nature, I couldn't get a revelation or discern what it was saying spiritually. It was still Logos and not Rhema, and I needed a word spoken into my spirit, which gave me the revelation of who God is. I wanted to know Him. Not a theologian's interpretation of Him.

For truly I thought I was saved, baptized, and almost filled with the Holy Spirit; later to realize that I really didn't know Jesus. That was my red Kool-Aid moment. My spirit was weak and my nature was strong. The Holy Ghost had not yet grown up filling this empti-ness residing in me, my house, my body. My temple was occupied by something else, called carnality. The residue of sin was still covering my mind. This was a religious thing to me, and I wasn't even close to understanding what a relationship was, especially with God. Oh, I gotta be real.

It was an action that we did over and over and over again. Some of us really believed that we were doing God a favor instead of being in His favor, and some just doing it because it seemed right, but there is a way that seems right to a man, but at the end of that way is death, or to make it plain, the devil. As 2 Timothy 3: 5 reads, having a form of godliness but denying the power thereof. You may hear me say this a few more times. But during a service, all that we do for the Lord is praise and worship. Teaching, preaching, and fellowshipping is for you, the congregation. The tithes are for the temple and the priest, and the offerings are for God's ministry to the needy, not the greedy.

A fugitive I was, running from a Father who loved me more than I loved myself.

God still had his hands on me, and He started to make it known too! No matter what the devil blinds you with, God can open your eyes, and God has a way of letting you know that He's coming back for what He has deposited in you. You see, He doesn't care about your religious affiliation or your spiritual disposition. For He has a way of moving. Moving you into preparation stages. For you must remember that your footsteps are ordered by the Lord. And you won't even know what's happening until the work is already done. Oh, He will allow your mind to be transformed instead of conformed. And when He's finished, the product that he presents Himself with will look like His son Jesus. Just like pure gold.

Here I was, finding myself running from the call of the Lord. Like a chicken with his head cut off. But if Jesus is your head, and you're running away from him, it makes you feel like such a hypocrite, such a fool; however, this is the situation I was in.

HANDCUFFED! TIED-UP!

I was thinking I could get away, but His arms are too long, and His jurisdiction is too great. You have to realize that at this time, I was twenty-one years of age. *I thought myself a young man full of vinegar,* in the prime of my life with so many opportunities that could have made me very rich and famous. For God placed in me the ability to create wealth and a lot of gifts that were very marketable in the world today. As you heard me say, in the world. That was my pimp. The truth is that I made a lot of other people very rich. About seven years ago, I sent in an invention that I pulled after me and my wife came to the belief that the agency wasn't up front with us about a lot of things. Just a little while ago, we saw that product on TV being marketed. Shows you how much you can trust the world, huh?

I was a martial artist who was very athletic. Sought after by a lot of people because of my skill. I was a professional kickboxer, a personal protection expert in a school where I was teaching a lot of people and I was working a full-time job in the same textile mill my father worked in. My work ethic was strong, and I wasn't lazy at all. Not that it made me rich, but it helped pay the bills. However, I let promoters use me to make their pockets thick. We were doing great as a family, but suddenly seemingly out of nowhere, my father was struck with a stroke that paralyzed him on one side. After this, not too many months later, my mother was diagnosed with diabetes that was so bad it forced her out of work. While I was serving the world, I lost sight of God's kingdom and got hung up in the world's way of doing things.

We slipped from the dimension of more-than-enough avenue to barely-getting-along boulevard. Hardship started setting in. It was like we were gonna spiral back down to the poverty level that we just climbed out of not too many years before. I understood what Mama was saying to me now when she said that life is filled with *ups* and *downs*. A recession had hit the land, and people were laid off and losing their jobs. The job where I was working went to slow time and cut a lot of hours out of the workweek. We worked one week and we were off one week. The karate Academy suffered from this because, my students couldn't even pay a thirty-dollar a month tuition. My kickboxing matches where I use to be guaranteed two fights per month, and a payday of at least eight hundred dollars per fight cut promotions because people weren't coming to the events. We were in a crisis.

I had a plan and a motivation but no direction, and this was a dangerous thing. I remember what I heard my pastor and spiritual father, Johnny O. Coe, said a long time ago (if you wanna make God laugh, just tell Him your plans. Either you can or you can't. Either you are or you ain't). My sisters and brothers were younger than me, and they depended on me. This was the motivating element which compelled me to take action. I took every fight I could get my hands on. Many were on short notice. Two or three days short notice. I'm glad I was in good condition. I worked all I could in the plant and in the proper season. I even worked in the fields too. At times, I was so tired that all I could do was fall in the bed to get some sleep. Momma got me to go back to church *after being out so long, focused on making money*. She said, "You need to be blessed, boy. Yes, we are in a bad place right now. But we've been through hard times before. Sometimes you may feel like we ain't gonna make it, but be patient with God 'cause He ain't through with you yet! Wait on the Lord and be of good courage. I say wait on the Lord!"

We were in church at least two times a week. Mom made sure we got there. One night, something very unsettling happened to me. I heard the voice of the Lord calling out to me, saying, "Lacy, why do you run from me?" It scared me so bad, I couldn't think straight. On the way home, I passed it off as my imagination and convinced myself that, yeah I'm just tired, that's what it is. I was misleading myself 'cause when you are without direction, you usually make the wrong decisions. When things start seemingly unreal to you, that's a spiritual attack. When something is stealing your joy, the devil is behind it.

To seek out wisdom at that time from an elder is a smart thing to do.

I was uneased, and even though my dad couldn't speak clearly, I had to talk to him. "Daddy," I said, "I'm tired, but I can't stop. I'm thinking about going to the army."

Daddy said, "No, boy, don't do that. I believe it's gonna be all right"!

Just that was enough to settle me down for a while, and it took a little stress off my mind. But I was not prepared for what was about to happen next.

Rev. Lacy and Emma Lee Green

3

MISLEAD

The next week, it seemed as if all hell broke loose. Job went bottoms up. People were laid off left and right. Well, I was one of them that was laid off this time, and that hurt. I was called back in a little while, but ouch! One week off could have bankrupted us. Living paycheck to paycheck was not a comfortable place to be, and *I don't wish that kind of survival training on anybody*. People fighting for a position on the job. Backstabbing their friends to find favor with the boss so they can work one more week!

Next, the PKA (Professional Karate Association), an international organization that sanctioned the full-contact fights, stopped using us small-town fighters. That hurt worse because I loved fighting, especially when I got paid for it. It helped me deal with the stress I was going through. And boy, was I going through!

Some months passed, and the struggle was still on, and as DMX said, "Ain't no sunshine went its on." Everyone was trying to pull their weight in work or support around the house, that is, those of us who were able. During this time, I spent more days around home. I closed my school down and started teaching in our garage to conserve money, and this kept a little money in the household, but I was a restless young man about this point. Though I had cut my overhead by closing the school, we still felt a great pinch. However, it felt as If I was connecting back with my true head, Jesus, 'cause He was the only one I could run to now. It's a crazy thing seeing how many only run to Jesus when they're in trouble. I started teaching my little brothers karate then. Wayne and Kenny 'cause we had lost Keith, and he went to be with the Lord. So I clung to my brothers that God left me with. This gave me a lot of joy. And I believed that this was a release for them also. We got closer and closer, and even today we can't be divided.

ENTER MISS EMMA TAYLOR

One day, I was invited to go to a parade in a town called Latta, which was about seven miles from Dillon, and I met the most beautiful girl. Her name was Emma. I had been introduced to her brother Luther a few months before, and we were good friends. Now, I was in love, but I was cool! I didn't want to move too fast. I wanted to see her, but I didn't have a car that was my own however. We started dating, and I found a way to get to her house. Bicycle, pat and Charlie—that's what we use to call walking—or I would get a close friend to take me over. But whether walking or hitchhiking, she was and still is worth every bit of the trouble. As a matter of fact, she was and still is a bless-ing. A virtuous woman worth her weigh in gold. Finer than precious jewels. It was she that made me rich.

The economy picked up a little, and in a little over a year, she became my wife, and my responsibilities got bigger. But still I was without any solid direction. I was playing my life by ear and my sight. Emma had to start work as a maid at Holiday Inn, and I didn't like that. Our first child was born a boy, and we named him Marcus Tyreme. Now I really had ants in my pants. I was dancing, jumping; my ego was lifted, and so was my spirit.

When I got to be twenty-three years old, my little brother Kenny flew the coop and joined the marines. I was scared for him because we were close, even though he was four years younger, but at least he would be getting a steady paycheck.

I needed to find something. I couldn't just stay in town barely making it. All I could see was my family in lack. However, every fam-ily was struggling. After about two years, my attention was caught by some advertisement on television, singing, "Be all that you can be 'cause we need you…in the *army*." So I decided to join the army, but the main reason was because in that commercial, it mentioned a five-thousand-dollar enlistment bonus. I saw my family coming out of this in my head. But at this time, I didn't know they would take half of it in taxes, and against my father's wishes, I joined the United States Army anyhow.

I played it smart as though I thought and joined the 82nd Airborne Division because it was close to my hometown. Wait a minute. I didn't want to ever be in the military. I was afraid of heights and really didn't want to jump out of a perfectly good airplane, and I didn't like people telling me what to do or bossing me around. Things that make you say *huh*. It's amazing what you will expect when you think it will get you out of a jam. And how many years you're willing to exchange for what you think would give you a little peace of mind.

I was assigned to Airborne Division Artillery, Combat Arms Artillery at Fort Bragg, North Carolina. That's what happens when you are without direction. You go where you didn't want to go, do what you didn't want to do, and be where you didn't want to be. Especially if you don't listen to your father, earthly or heavenly, you can make your bed very hard to lie in. But all things work together for the good of those that love Him and are called to His purpose.

Life is like a game of checkers. You have to do a little thinking before you make your next moves, or you could lose or waste it by giving it over to somebody other than God. God placed me in a learning environment where I had to listen and be governed by somebody. Some were younger than I was, and sometimes that really pissed me off because they made some bad decisions. Sounds familiar, doesn't it? However, they were in a position that they had the authority to make that decision. I had to submit myself under that authority. Because a man without direction is like a misguided missile. You don't know where you're gonna wind up or where you may blow up or self-destruct. I remember in the movie *Forrest Gump* where his mother told him, "Life is like a box of chocolates, you never know what you're gonna get."

Well, enough about that in this segment; however, can I let you know something? Though bad things were happening, God still was watching over me. I didn't know it, and a lot of times, it didn't feel good. But it was working out for my good. The Father was teaching me lessons to build me up. My character was still lacking and in some areas even twisted, but He didn't want to break my spirit, just aided me in controling my flesh.

I know God has a sense of humor 'cause He created me as He created all, and He will take you away from your support system, your comfort zone, to make you know that you got to lean on Him. And now He orders the directions for my footsteps. He guides my path and leads me into all righteousness and understanding through His Son Jesus. He is my only Source. My Ya-havah Yirei.

God my provider.

Things That I've learned

1. My core belief is that God doesn't change his mind about your purpose. He changes things, circumstances, and situations surrounding you to direct you to His desired effect or His plan for your life. He means it for your good. It's confusing when He does this, but He gives you a revelation about what strings He is pulling, what doors He is opening or closing, and the people that He brought in your life, whether for a season or for a lifetime, to shape and mold you. Many theologians only know God by a collaborated study of places, happening, and things that are written on the tablets we call the Bible. Or reports of miraculous things, and they try to draw conclusion about who He is, but there is no conclusion to Him, and the only way to truly know Him is if you write His word in your heart and through personal experiences with Him. For we are finite, but He is infinite. You can't put Him in a box. He won't be contained in your little book or anything of the type.

The humor about this is God knew to call me when I was young because I was hardheaded, thought I knew everything, and I was gonna run from anyone who tried to get me to do what I didn't what to do and cover my ears so I wouldn't hear what He was saying. So He sent me to where I could only hear, man's orders, do what I didn't want to, even down to taking up guns and shooting at people, while they were shooting at me. But my savior Jesus is a Master Fisherman and knows where the fish are. He couldn't catch me when I was nonmilitary. I was listening to too many people. So he caught me in the military where I got tired of listening to people and started listening to His voice and longing for Him to speak to me and tell me what to do to get out of the mess I had gotten myself into. But if Jesus is a Master Fisherman, God is the Master of masters.

2. Being without direction can lead you down a road of self-destruction, or you can wind up going around in circles, *just like the children of Israel,* who wandered in the desert around the mountain for forty years. God can put you on probation. Now I seek His direction, I seek His counsel, and I seek His wisdom for dealing with the obstacles that Satan has placed in the way. You need a master navigator to make it through the minefields.

3. You are not your own man! Somebody is pulling the strings. I got tired of fooling myself thinking that very same thing that I was my own man. But if I was my own man calling my own shots, I would be rich, have new cars. I would control my health, all my family would be saved, and know where I was going and end up. But though the Father gives us freedom, a lot of times, we have to ask permission. Can you help me? Is it in your will? Thy will be done. No, God is in control, unless you are a rebel, as I was, and then the adversary is in control, and you are then a rebel without a cause. Jesus paid the cost to be our boss.

I was acting out a part. The truth is that I didn't know where I was going; fleshly voices that catered to the devil's bidding were jerking me around. I am so thankful that God had the stronger pull. He showed me that the path He had chosen for me was not gonna be a walk in the park. He toughened me for this journey. So I humbled myself and submitted to His guidance, and God turned things around. Now I know I will make it to my destination.

Kyoshi Kenny Green Lacy's little brother
United States Marine Corps, retired 1988

Captain Kenny Green is now a federal prison officer working in South Carolina. Still a superior martial artist and teacher of war angels TZK Martial Arts Academy. I'm very pleased that my brothers are so successful in life. And to know that they love the Lord as much as I, founder of the MATT (martial arts tournament tours) and the PPKF (Professional Point Karate Federation).

Lacy in a promotion ceremony with his
little brother Shihan Wayne Green

Wayne Wendell Green, retired sheriff detective and superior martial artist. Chief instructor of War Angels TZK Martial Arts Academy. He is the baby brother every big brother wished they had. Founded the quartets second chance. Actor in hometown, plays now owner of the PPKF.

4

WITHOUT A PERSONAL RELATIONSHIP WITH MY SAVIOR

As we navigate through the roadmaps and the troubled waters of life, we come to the realization that we are natural creatures. Natural creatures with natural needs and desires that will quickly lead us to sin or shortcomings, for we are born into it, and many pursue it because it takes no effort to find it. But anything worth finding takes a little effort. Man is a threefold being. Man is a spirit who lives in a body and possesses a soul.

Things that are bad for us but seem good to us are usually the downfall of us. They become readily available, and the temptation to commit sin in them or with them is right around every corner. It's easy to find because it stays on your mind. Things like sex, drugs, and rock and roll. But let us examine one that may hold tight to all of our minds: sex! This is a subject that makes it hard, for a man, to tread water. Oh no, I'm not forgetting about you, ladies. Because it's many of you that make it hard for men to tread water. Ah, y'all don't love me no more, do you?

This is where many people stand when it comes to gender, male or female. Some think it's a way to show that they are grown-up so they fornicate, commit adultery, and other foolish sins of the flesh. Some think even though they're married to one, because of ungodly counsel while growing up, they believe that it's all right if they had one on the side. A second one to commit adultery with, and are not loyal or faithful in any of their relationship because they don't fix the problem! Oh, did I say that too loudly? Okay then. When you write your book, you can write as loud as you want to! Cheating is the norm these days, no trust in your mate, and no consideration for a person's feelings.

The devil has perverted the commitment between male and female! I say this for the ones who know beyond a shadow of a doubt what they are! Some are confused, and that perverts even the divine order, foundation, and institution of marriage. Lesbians and homosexual marriages are now on the rise, and the states, courts, and laws of the land are deciding whether to allow or disallow it. Loyalty in the relationships of man and woman is based on instructions given by God. Some are so bold, or should I say twisted, because they want to defile themselves with the same gender. I love men too, but I'm sorry, not like that! Oh, preacher, hush, your mouth!

Somewhere on this journey, we've heard a voice crying out, and it was the voice or the Lord calling unto a lost soul, saying, come to me and out of your slavery to the flesh and be saved. No, no, I didn't stutter. But there was another voice telling you to do the opposite. And that voice is the devil's, Satan's, the anti-Christ's. Everyone has this wrestling with their carnality.

No matter who planted the seed of waywardness in us, it took root. But the truth is that even from birth, you would do wrong without any help because we are born in iniquity. Somebody just watered it, and then come, yeah, the increase. Sin never decreases on its own. It only escalates more and more. Sin in your life can be a heavy burden, and that yoke around your neck can drag you to the deepest depth, drowning you. It is the instrument that the devil uses to lead many to destruction. No one is exempted from this. They will be teased, tempted, and finally, tested. But never by God, but by the enemy. There has to be somebody there so you could hear and see what was right and what was wrong.

But the knowledge of it has to bring about a willingness to change. No one is in there stronger than our flesh until we find Jesus. Like a moth drawn to the flame of a candle, we're drawn to *sin*. I *say again*, every man has a working knowledge of what is right and what is wrong, and there is a constant war going on between your flesh and your spirit man for your soul. Oh, and you thought the devil made you do it, huh! *No*, he's only the influence of a bad idea. You make the choice to take the action. But if you lift Jesus up, He will draw all men unto Him.

Your flesh is considered to be your natural drawing, or what some call *instinct*. That's what we associate with animal behavior, lust, or wild passion, but the reasoning ability of the human sets a higher standard of morality because of defiance in the Garden of Eden, we are apt to do evil even when that still small voice tells us to do good. And we can be persuaded to do opposite of what our Father commanded us to do. The mind or soul has to be changed, and that's in the way that we think.

We are the sons of the first Adam before we truly become the sons of God and what God has planted in us. The attraction to a male or female has been twisted in the thorns and weeds that the devil made to grow in our ground or soulish realm. So when it comes to the flesh, we tend to write our own bible, our own little books, on the subject of how to behave. For instance, if the preferred relationship is of a homosexual or gay type, the process is that of beating down any belief or institution that preaches or speaks against it. It is attacked with resistance and extreme prejudice. We take the philosophy of if "it feels good, do it" or anything that feels so good has to be good. Lying to ourselves and, as with any sexual sin that is unlawful in the eyes of God, sinning against our soul.

We proclaim ourselves as god because we want to do what we want to do. Our actions, our money, and our lives are tangled up in physical satisfaction, and this is what consumes the entire thinking process of the individual. We become a reprobate. Thinking we can do no wrong. Thinking anything we do is right 'cause we want it to be. Rebelling against what is right is the way of the evil one, and there we go acting like the devil.

Some even become obsessed with it to the point of incapacitation. They can't work, can't eat, can't sleep, and sexually harassing, rapes, pornography, and more skyrockets across the nation and

around the world. These are the ones who close their minds to changing because this is their religion. This is their world; we're just squirrels trying to get a nut. But the only reward they receive is sin and death. I refuse to be so reluctant to change and be stagnated in sin, stuck in a world where the only reward is death and judgement. Obsessed by the abomination of unbridled lust. And lust of an unnatural kind is definitely off-limits, out of the question. Taking the position of a sodomite is a filthy thing. But if there is anyone out there who really wants to change any sexual perversion, God is still God, and He is the Judge, and yes, He still loves you. Repent and return!

We may think that we are all that and a bag of chips. But it's not about us, it's Jesus. Because Jesus has already come, and he's coming again. God sent us the answer; now we have to receive him. Because the enemy can still rip our souls away if we allow it. The lust of the eye, lust of the flesh, and pride of life drives all that is in the world, and we are accustomed to rubbing elbows with the devil or Baal every day. In this chapter, I hit a little harder, but I never knew the devil to hit soft. And you don't cuss him out, do you? Many are closer to him than to God. So how do we create a right relationship with ourselves and with God? As David says, "Lord, create in me a right spirit." To do this, we have to return to the Genesis (the beginning of things). The order of first things in the book of Genesis is it returns to Adam and Eve. But even before that was the relationship between God and Adam. The relationship between a man and a woman. God ordained this in divine order; however, the first love or relationship is between God and man, not of a sexual type, but agape, a godly kind of love and relationship. A relationship between creator and creation. I can't say that enough.

Genesis travels in two parts: The first is being the universal creation, rebellion, punishment, and restoration. That sounds a lot like marriage, doesn't it?

1. The creation of a union is a contract written in blood.
2. The rebellion is from not being loyal or faithful, submitting yourselves one to another. This is hard to do if you are not equal.

3.   The punishment of separation or divorce. Not being able to trust each other, get along, or come to an agreement or willingness to work through any of the problems that complicates a union.

4.   And the restoration. Many times, this doesn't happen with the same person unless some forgiveness and love is put in the mix. Usually, the restoration in this instance pertains to a healing of the heart and soul, a strengthening of the injured person and the ability to move forward. All in all, Jesus is there to restore the relationship between God and man. This has to be fixed before any relationship works.

But where this model differs is that many times in a troubled relationship, many of us never restore the union with the same person, as I said before. I think that deserves being repeated. See, we jump right to the next. This maybe some of our intentions in the beginning. However, there are many families or unions that stay together as in the second part. God chose a particular family to bless the nations or ethnicities. This is the example. A relationship is a covenant, and a marriage is a blood covenant, especially with a virgin or maiden. In a world like today, there is no commitment, and we find couples cohabitating or shacking up, as they used to call it. But I understand that to get married is a big thing because it takes two to begin a marriage and only one to end it. If the person wants no part of his or her mate, the union is a disaster any way. However, you must repent for your part in it.

Human reflection upon this book from the point of origin onward has not completely been understood. Its theological richness and its call to covenant, faithfulness, and hope are confusing to the majority of us. Human sin inspired by the evil act to destroy it has now become the driving force of the sons of ungodliness set to taint a natural function of human procreation.

Satan's scheme to defile the bloodline of the Messiah brought divine judgement, resulting in this world age of pain, labor, and frustration we now experience. Our rebellion gave Satan the control over us, and he manipulates the thinking of man or twists it so an unredeemed soul is led into acting out impulsive thoughts, and many of them are vile and repulsive, unnatural, and an abomination to divine order. Many act as Jesus said, "Like your father, the devil." This gets a lot deeper, but I don't want to go into this now.

But God's grace and mercy has a way of redeeming the vilest offender. It's almost like God needs to have a relationship with us, as much as we need to have a relationship with Him. He is our Father, and He loves us, and He created us, no matter what some may try to blow up your tail pipe because despite differences of opinions, I don't look like no monkey! And evolution has no place in my vocabulary. It's just a theory, but I know the truth.

I feel like we owe it to God to get in right standing, with a right relationship with Him and our brother, with male and female, with man and animal, for we all have this connection to one supreme source, and He is God Ya-havah. Jesus said, "How is it that you say you love God who you haven't seen and hate your brother who you see every day?" So relationship with God has to begin first by showing Him your good relationship with your friends, your enemies, your wife, your children, your sisters and brothers, your leaders, etc. And all right relationships begins with love. And I will exit this chapter by leaving you with this verse from Corinthians: "Love is patient and kind: love doesn't envy. Love doesn't brag, is not proud, doesn't behave itself inappropriately, doesn't seek its own way, is not provoked, takes no account of evil; doesn't rejoice in unrighteousness, but rejoices with the truth; bears all things, believes all things hopes all things, endures all things. Love never fails" (1 Corinthians 13:4-8).

5

WITHOUT LOVE AND DEVOTION

"For God so loved the world that he gave His only begotten son. That who so ever believeth in him shall not perish but have everlasting life" (John 3:16). I love this scripture and remember it always, for I realize that many have forgotten what real love and devotion is. They have forgotten the Lamb who was slain for the sins of man and who is our Passover, our covering from the sting of death and the victory over the grave. For He is the resurrection and has shown us the way to everlasting life, for he who is dead and believeth in Him shall live again, but he who liveth and believeth in Him shall never die. And I want to live forever. How about you? I'm looking forward to that transitioning. Taking off the mortal and putting on the immortal.

This chapter will be filled with scriptures and sayings in the attempt to make and define differences between true love and infatuation. Many of us remember when we were little, and we saw a little girl or boy we liked, we would write a letter, and it read "I love you. Do you love me? Mark yes or no." If the answer was *yes,* you probably were goo-goo eyed for about a week, then the next week, you or they would be writing another letter to another little boy or little girl. Now we are grown, and we base love on the same concept. An outward appearance, a pretty face, a muscular body, classy clothes, a zodiac sign, so on and so forth. But this scripture shows what real love is. It's about giving, not taking, as some of us believe and practice every day. When we've taken all that we wanted, we discard it. Love goes a lot deeper than that. And when we can dig deep enough, then we may get to truly know what John 3:16 is talking about. Let us take a look at some of the verses from the Bible that speaks of love and see if we can get a better understanding of this. But first, let's take a little detour.

Some of us remember the love songs that we listened to when we were younger, and we may still hear them from time to time. But every song that had the word *love* in it wasn't speaking about true and unconditional love. The kind of love that makes you tell your mate, "Baby, you look good right now, but even if you go cockeyed tomorrow, I'll still love you," or "Sweetheart, I love you and all your muscles, but I don't care if you get a beer belly next week, I'll still love you," or "Dear, I love every curl on your head, but if you go bald tomorrow, I'll still love you. Even if your teeth fall out or you don't have no money." No. Most of our love is based on appearance, convenience, or stability. Infatuation or lustful sexual love is more predominant in our society today than true unadulterated love.

Love is defined in the *Holman Bible Dictionary* as unselfish, loyal, and benevolent, concerned for the well-being of another. If we were being graded on this definition, the majority of us would receive a zero, for we fail to forget about self and to remember loyalty and well-being of another. To understand John 3:16, we see that God was not selfish with His son. He is always loyal to His creation and always holds our well-being into consideration. He didn't forget about us because we had sinned. He worked it out so we could come to Him again as a righteous one through His son Yeshuwa, Jesus our Messiah, even though we went whoring after other gods and forsake our relationship with Him, our first love.

Paul describes love as a more excellent way, but let's not get it twisted. What he is saying is that agape, that God kind of love is excellent. Not eros or philia, which are the other two types or breakdowns of love, and I mean breakdowns.

Eros: love is of physical pleasure and satisfaction.
Philia: love is between parents and children, or of like unions.

The word says in the last days, man shall be lovers of themselves instead of lovers of God!

Some play love like a game, and that's how many get their hearts broken, and some even scarred for life with emotional damages that hinder their trust, rendering them of no effect, not able to truly love again. When I saw this in me is when I turned in my playa card. In a relationship such as this, there was one taker and one giver, one player and one being played, one who was selfish and one selfless. Which one are you? The user or the one being used? Very seldom are these relationships fifty—fifty because they're not based on a true foundation.

It's either-or, "take and no give," or "all give and no take." The Bible tells us to guard our hearts, and in so doing, we must understand that the enemy pollutes and contaminates an unguarded heart. You must know about all three types of love in order to know which one is the counterfeit. In this you will understand how God loves you. Then you will be able to love yourself and then love others. Finding out that the devil doesn't love you.

Someone long ago sung a song called, "Love Is a Many Splendid Thing," and true love or agape is truly a splendid thing. So always remember that Satan has us in a ringer, and he's always trying to twist how we think. Perversion in our mind can send us in a downward descent to the lowest levels of possible existence. Here is where we may become obsessed, depressed, and/or possessed. For not understanding the real meaning or purpose of love can leave your mind messed up, your body messed up, and eventually your life messed up. Many times I've felt like I was tore up from the floor up, beat-up from the feet up, and messed-up from the chest up, as I've said a while ago.

When many of us were younger, we took love as a simple sexual or physical thing. But true love is supernatural or spiritual and transcends all physical reality.

Love has to be bigger than a physical thing or an attraction thing, a visual thing, or even a mental thing. It has to be a heart thing and even a spiritual thing, a gift of God thing, or else one may find that they are even lying to themselves. Played a fool by vanity and vainness or even unnatural lust, and such is sinful. You may find yourself looking for love in all the wrong places, and confusion will dominate your decision-making process, and flirtations of carnal individuals will entice you. Curiosity will control your actions, and just as curiosity kills the cat, the counterfeit will kill your heart, making it callous and unable to feel what is real. Emotions will go crazy, and you will make some of your most regrettable mistakes.

One of the most powerful revelations that God gave me came while I was doing research on the sinful nature. It will take or move you out of place or out of position because your actions will be out of order. Just as when the fallen angels left their post and followed the devil. Many fall victim to this because of their lack of knowledge on this subject, and it becomes rebellion against the purpose of God for their life. God can't bless you because you tie His hands. Being led by the natural man, we will find ourselves being fornicators and adulterers and whoremongers following a perverted spirit that will take us down a road of destruction, where people live on the low-down. Homosexuality, lesbianism, rape, child molestation, and incest could find you on this road. This road will take you to the end of life or lake of fire. This is just a brief paragraph of sexual sin that God says in His word: if a man commits them, he sins against his own soul, and no matter how I try to look at it, it doesn't seem like you love yourself if you sin against your own soul.

A person who loves his or herself would want to have their soul saved rather than go to the lake of fire. We as natural men have a tendency to use things until we're tired of it and throw it away, as I said before, and that's why we discard or divorce one another. In a real relationship, there is devotion. Devotion is a word that means a strong attachment or affection to a person or cause. We dilute that meaning, for we are moderately attached and moderately affectionate, which is so easy to walk away from. Especially when things aren't going your way.

Some of us walk away from God in the same manner, but to know about that God kind of love, you must first know God and develop personal relationship with Him through prayer, praise, and worship, which develops devotion or a need to stay attached, and through that relationship, you will understand that though you may have messed up, God still loves you enough to lift you up. Even before you were conceived, He knew you, and He made so many deposits in your life so that your purpose would be fulfilled. Are you gonna fumbling the ball? Are you gonna screw it up? Or will you fight to be right?

So in loving God, I've truly learned to love people, and at the same time, I press toward my purpose in Him. There were so many years that I chased after my flesh rather than walk in His spirit, whoremongering, thinking I was God's gift to women, half-man, half-amazing. I talked to women so smoothly that they thought I invented sex, but I was a curse to many of them, and for this, I've repented many times; however, I really dishonored my Father God and became His enemy without even knowing it. Following the norm instead of following the Spirit of God. I'm so glad He restored me and resurrected my lost years; atonement has been made, and now I can love Him as he deserves to be loved, devoting myself totally and submitting my will to Him.

Father! I love ya! With all that is within me, for you are a magnificent God. Excellent in all your ways and awesome to behold. Heaven and earth are full of your glory. I praise your holy name, Ya-havah, for you are the only reason that I exist. By feeling this way, God has released power in my life, my marriage, and in my actions in the form of His precious Holy Spirit.

If I were to testify about His grace and mercy, I would have to confess that He is a protector, a healer, a deliverer, a provider, a peacemaker, and, oh yes, He's everything to me. I am an overcomer by the blood of Jesus and the work of the Holy Spirit in my life. God has done great things in me, and I refuse to be without love for Him and my fellowmen, and a devotion to the service of ministry in which He has called me to. For in order to perform the great commission, you must first have love for people and be devoted to the success and accomplishment of winning souls.

Let's just look at some verses that are about love:

Ephesians 2:4–6: "But God, who is rich in mercy, for his great love where with He loved us. Even when we were dead in sins, hath quicken us together with Christ. (By grace ye are saved;) and hath raised us up together and made us sit together in heavenly place in Christ Jesus…"

1 John 4:19: "We love Him, because He first loved us."

John 15:13: "Greater love has no one than this that one lay down his life for his friends."

These are great verses and very simple to understand, but one that I revere is Psalm 145:20:

"The Lord preserveth all them that love Him: but all the wicked will He destroy."

Romans 12:9–10: "Love must be sincere, hate what is evil; Cling to what is good. Be devoted to one another in brotherly love. Honor one another above yourselves."

1 John 4:7–8: "Beloved let us love one another: for love is of God, and every one that loveth is born of God, and knoweth God. He that loveth not knoweth not God, for God is Love."

These verses are great to give you the insight you need to discern one love from the other. But there is a flip side of the coin called lust. Let's look at what God has to say about it.

Oh, you better run now 'cause this gets all of us.

2 Timothy 2:22 says, "Flee also youthful lusts; but follow righteousness, faith, charity, and peace, with them that call on the Lord out of a pure heart."

Proverbs 6: 25, 27–29 says, "Do not lust in your heart after her beauty or let her captivate you with her eyes…Can a man scoop fire into his lap without his clothes being burned? Can a man walk on hot coals without his feet being scorched? So is he who sleeps with another man's wife; No one who touches her will go unpunished.

1 Thessalonians 4:4 says, "That each of you should learn to control his own body in a way that is holy and honorable, not in passionate lust like the heathen, who do not know God…"

These are just a few verses out of many, but very powerful. I hope you can see some of what I'm trying to tell you. My life is an open book. I've made so many mistakes. When I committed my life to the Lord, I was so sorrowful for what I had done I had to talk with my mother about it. I said, "Momma, I messed up. I feel sick to my soul about it." I'll never forget what she told me. She said, "Lace, everybody messes up sometimes, you'll fall down in the mud. But you don't have to wallow in it! So I'll leave you with this. Beauty is only skin-deep, ugliness is to the bone. When beauty dies and fades away, ugliness holds its own. Sin, lust, and everyone who commits sins of the flesh will be here even after you're dead and gone from this realm of existence. Will you let what is temporary in this age end your living in His Kingdom the next age and forever?" As I said before, I, my wife, and my children chose life eternal. Nothing here is worth losing eternity for.

6

WITHOUT A PRAISE

After all that we have done that was not according to God's word. I feel all would be a waste if we had no purpose. Thank God that he has revealed it to us at the simplest form, for our purpose first of all is to please Him. And I believe that there is something about our praise that God loves. No matter how hard times may get, he is a fool who believes God has never done anything for them that is worthy of praise.

John 3:16 is a great reminder of how much He has given us because of His love. "For God so loved the world, that He gave His only begotten son, that whosoever believeth in him should not perish, but have everlasting life." I always give honor to *the Father*. Almighty God, Adoni, El-shidai, the many-breasted one and to Jesus, Yeshuwa, His only-begotten son our Lord, who shed his blood so that we could have a chance at everlasting life.

It is truly a privilege to stand before anyone and proclaim the name of the most high. Because the hunger is there for the truth. Every now and then, people need to cry out, "Lord, feed me!" There is something about our praise, that God loves. Because He inhabits the very praises of his people. That means the more you praise, the closer He gets. For He is a Mighty God, and we enter His gates with thanksgiving and enter His courts with praise.

There is none like Him. For He is Spirit, and those that worship Him must do so in spirit and in truth. I believe the book of Psalms has the most to say about praise. But talking about it and really doing it are two different things. Praise is totally physical, where worship is 90 percent spiritual. Praise confuses the enemy because he can't understand why we still have our joy. As Psalm 71:7–8 reads, "I am a marvel to many, but you are my strong refuge. My mouth shall be filled with your praise, with your honor all the day."

Now my heart is full of praise for he has opened up my eyes, and I am not like a blind man anymore. I know the truth, and my trust is in Him. You see, when I couldn't stand on my own, he supported me. When I was sick, He healed me. When I was in a strange land in combat for the USA, He protected me. What a mighty God we serve. Magnificent in all His ways. That's why I know He is worthy to be praised. Just to be able to call on Him is worth the praise. So many have turned their backs on Him because of some issue in their lives.

But into every life, a little rain must fall. Everyone goes through. It's how you handle yourself while you're going through that's important. *I have to say this.* Some of us are big crybabies. We have to cuss and fuss, make excuses, jump up and down, throw a tantrum, anything to show our discontents. While the devil stands back and laughs at us.

You're saying, "How come I have it so bad? Oh poor is me, woe is me." If you're in a fix, it's time to get a hold of yourself and fight you way out of it! The devil loves a wimp! Oh, now it ain't funny no more, is it? It's a slap in the face, an insult to who you really are! Sometimes you got to get mad enough with that sucka' to declare war. But after you do that, you have to be equipped with the right weapons to fight with. Praise is one of the best weapons you got. Prayer, the word, the name of *Jesus* are three more, but praise is very important because that's what will bring Him close to you, even in your corner. For He inhabits even the praises of His people.

You may think, *What is this persecution all about?* See, you don't win with a lot of fussing and cussing. You receive your victory through your praise. That alone makes the adversary look stupid.

Psalm 42:5, 11:43, 5:45, 17:71, 14 are just a few of the scriptures that speak of praise. They read:

> Psalm 42:11: "Why art thou cast down, O my soul? And why thou disquieted within me? Hope thou in God: for I shall yet praise him, who is the heath of my countenance, and my God."

> Psalm 45:17: "I will make thy name to be remembered in all generations: therefore shall the people praise thee forever and ever."

> Psalm 71:14: "But I will hope continually, and will yet praise thee more and more."

Oh, I wonder is there anybody out there with a praise yet? A praise that you can say it doesn't matter what's going wrong in my life, *yet* will I praise Him! My soul is so happy just because He considered me to be His son. I remember *how I strived to please* my earthly father before he transitioned to heaven. I loved him so much. And to think of all the things my heavenly Father did to make room for me in His kingdom is phenomenal. I can't explain it, and my mind can't contain it. For I could have been as one who is blotted out of the book of the living. I feel like David in Psalm 69:16, "Hear me, *O Lord ; for they lovingkindness is good; turn unto me according to the multitude of thy tender mercies."*

God is good, and as the church folks say: all the time. I am a living witness to that fact. The manifestation of His grace and mercy brought me through. One verse at a time. There is a verse that says that His grace and mercy follow me. Maybe that's the reason I didn't get cut off! Maybe that's the reason we've made it so far. For His grace empowers me to overcome sin. I used to struggle to get a praise out. Now I can't keep one in. As my mother used to say, "He's so good to me, I just can't keep it to myself. I got to tell somebody about the goodness of the Lord!" Man, did she know what she was talking about. I refuse to be without a praise.

*Oh somebody better talk
to me up in here!*

I still have the use of my hands, my arms, my legs, my feet. He opened my eyes so I can see, and I'm not a blind man any more bumping against things that I shouldn't even touch.

It's so important to me to give this thing of myself. For if I can do nothing else, I can present myself as a living sacrifice, holy and acceptable to God, which is my reasonable service or ministry. By making this sacrifice, I return a part of this life he has given me for the price that he paid for me on Calvary. So praise is what I do to show my gratitude, my appreciation, my overwhelming love for my Father and His Son. Because they worked it out for me. I like to personalize this fact at times 'cause I don't know what you came to do. But I came to praise the Lord. And I refuse to be without a praise.

7

OTHER THAN

I decided to make this chapter stand out in your spirit in order to create a change, for I know that some who would read this might have problems discerning which way to go, or may need encouragement to keep going, or be motivated to continue pressing on in the right direction. Sometimes labor pains increase to give us the means to push forward.

Life is not easy, and in this journey, we will have lots of ups and downs, but thanks be to God for the ups, and thank Him for the downs as well! For without the ups, we would become discouraged, but without the downs, our faith wouldn't have matured, and if we hadn't exercised it, we would still be weak in faith. This is what makes us strong enough to grab a hold of His promises. Your faith must stand the trials or test of time, and you'll never know how strong your faith is until you're in a good fight.

So there are a lot of things I refuse to be, but there is a flip side to that statement, and that is...*other than*. But what am I to be, who will I be, what should I be because life is a state of being, living, existing on this planet at this time. What am I to be or become?

We were made for a time such as this, and as William Shakespeare asked the famous question, "To be or not to be." We ask that same question day in and day out. So I have some other statements that may further join our minds together, for this is the soul of man, and many of us must change our way of thinking. For let this mind be in you which was also in Christ Jesus. Many will live the life of the man who walks under the sun, this is the carnal or natural man, but we should walk the life of the man who truly owns this temple called the body, which is the spirit man. For by walking in him and in the Spirit of God, we won't satisfy the lust of the flesh, which is filled with selfishness, treachery, hatred, deceitfulness, and malice.

I refuse to be other than concerned for the well-being of God's creations, especially my brother man, but also for the animals not like us, but so much like us, for we share the same space, and all have their purpose. Also plants, for they have their own purpose, for God gave us dominion over them, not to destroy them but to cultivate and help them flourish. Not to drive them to extinction but to carry them until the end.

A reconciliation to the Father cannot take place unless we first realize who we are and whom we are. We are the sons of God, the caretakers, His children, the stewards of his masterpiece, planet earth and all its inhabitants. Because we as Gentiles were grafted into the promises of Abraham; by adoption, we should carry our light higher and shine brighter because of that fact. For we were wayward, not considering the consequences of our rebellious nature. It's a blessing to know that God still loves us enough as not to disown or discard us as a worthless piece of flesh, not good for anything except destruction.

I refuse to be other than a servant of mankind everywhere. For to just be concerned about the people in your household, people in your community, people of your ethnic persuasion, nationality, or religious belief is a cop-out to me and a lessening of our responsibility because you don't want to be responsible. You are your brother's keeper. Not like Cain who was his brother's murderer.

Sometimes we get people in control or overpower who have a legitimate desire to make a difference, but because of the politics of the people surrounding them, it ties their hands, and their time in power is of little effect. For example, at this time, I believe we have a true president who is concerned about his people, as a good king is concerned about his subjects. That president is President Barak Obama, and I believe if many of us don't wake up and support him to the fullest, pray for him and our congress, we may miss the opportunity to live for many years stress-free.

About some issues that plague us today, we can have debates, but to delay and tie someone's hands by filibuster or coping out is not the way to do something that is needed. For many needed health care insurance that couldn't afford it yesterday, and I'm talking about twenty years ago and will die before their time because of the greed of greedy men who say we don't want a government-sponsored health insurance. Well, give us another one affordable and effective, for the ones that are available are pushing hardworking people to bankruptcy. Who are they speaking for anyway? They say that the people don't want a government-controlled insurance. I believe they are talking about the ones who pay for their reelection campaign, and we as a needy people fall for the smoke screen and can't see through their deception or lying. Some don't even know what is best for them. How can they know what is best for us?

I know many who need help. For this type of reasoning is suspect since the Republican agenda is only to fill their own pockets or keep them full. This is a childish ploy, and just like kids, they're playing, putting on a mask looking concerned when we know they won't be affected either way with this. They have more than they may ever need and still storing up. Geared to hoard money and not save lives. Already. It has increased tenfold because of a war we didn't order, and if this issue would have been addressed thirty years ago, it would've been a lot of *taxpayers money wasted*! Now it's time to take care of our people to assist them in living instead of sending many to their death, for war can only do that.

People who are rich care little about the poor. Their charity is wax cold, and I believe many of them have no God in them. They are hypocrites, playing a role on a worldwide stage. For many are selfish and have the attitude of I, I, me, me, and my, my. I have a lot of things to say about this, but that is another book. But anyway, I say God raises up a king. It is our job to pray for them, not fight them every step of the way.

How could we have come so far together and still be so far apart in the way we think? Jesus told us that the poor we would have with us always. Now I can see why. The hearts of men are not really sincere about helping their brothers up. Many of us *fight to hold them down.* Many of us are concerned, but many are greedy and only think about possessing all we want, which is well above what we need. They have a crab mentality that pulls down anyone who may gain a foothold above them. Speaking of the final chapter: is this where we stall, or will we gain some forward momentum and start trying to fix that what is broken? Everyone has their own issues. A group is against this, and another for that. But usually, this is just a smoke screen to keep us blinded from the things that are truly important. We call this majoring in the minors, which helps nobody. It's just procrastinating.

The prophet Isaiah spoke of a time such as this when the men in power would act like children. In the third chapter: "For, the Lord, the *lord of host,* doth take away from Jerusalem and from Judah the stay and the staff, the whole stay of bread, and the whole stay of water, The mighty man, and the man of war, the judge, and the prophet, and the Prudent, and the ancient, The captain of fifty, and the honorable man, and the counselor, and the cunning artificer, and the eloquent orator. And I will give children to be their princes, and babes shall rule over them" (Isa 3:1–4).

And our congress and senate are acting just like that. It's becoming a popularity contest instead of doing what is right for the country's people process. The more I look at it, I believe that they want to take the food and the ability to get it from the needy. And more people will steal to feed their babies, which will lead to more killing and all this other crazy junk that's happening around us.

Fear is the game that people play. And in this endgame, we have only one answer: Jesus. Time has gone by, and now I'm positioned for His purpose. However, this was a long process. Thank God my direction is true, and my calling sure. Blessed be the name of the Lord. For I live in His kingdom instead of the kingdom of children and fools who hold up progress and play a waiting game where people die to prove their point! Where mammon or Baal is their god, they hand us counterfeit tickets that serve no one.

For the enemy comes to kill, steal, and destroy. But I am come that you may have life and have it more abundantly. Amazingly, life has been good to me. Despite where I came from, God has smiled on me. For the I am come.

There is a scripture, Luke 54:45–49 and the word of God reads: "Then opened he their understanding, that they might understand the scripture. And said unto them, thus it is written, and thus it behooved Christ to Suffer, and to rise from the dead the third day; And that repentance and remission of sins should be preached in his name among all nations, beginning at Jerusalem. And ye are witnesses of these things. And, behold, I send the promise of my Father upon you; but tarry ye in the city of Jerusalem, until ye be endued with power from on high."

And because (the I am come) I now walk in the power of the Holy Spirit. How many times in your life have you desired to do something that at the time seemed virtually impossible? Can you count the times even in this past year that circumstances and situations almost overpowered you, taking your strength, rendering you seemingly powerless? Where you get caught up between a rock and a hard place about ready to throw in the towel because you feel there is no hope.

Why does it feel like it's so hard to live a victorious life as a spirit-born believer when you've heard the word and believed it? Because the devil don't like it when you're dressed like that. You might not think so, but you are special. And I know that it doesn't feel like it sometimes. But you have been empowered from on high, and the adversary doesn't like it. Where the adversary is, there is adversity. You can't get comfortable because things are constantly changing. And you have to stay on your toes so he won't catch you unaware.

He's an impatient being who suffers from anxiety, and he wants you to fall, and not just fall, but fall quickly. *But* just keep resisting; he will run away because he can't stand a challenge. For when you resist, you have developed the power to rebuke him in the name of Jesus. *Raising* a standard, a rule, a measure that is beyond reproach.

Levels to This Christian Walk

There are levels to our Christian walk. This journey will lead us into a higher level of understanding and depending on what you are being fed or what you're eating from the table, the altar, or that which the man of God is speaking or teaching. First, you drink milk, then you eat meat, but at this buffet, you have to learn to eat it all a little at a time. Which brings us to another dilemma. The reason why many of us are not higher in the Lord is because we're either malnourished or we don't want to grow up. Our teeth have not yet cut through the gums. Are we still playing church? After all this time, are we still babies, drinking milk who won't touch the meat? Some of us are even lactose intolerant, and they can't even tolerate the milk and be faithful with that. Their desire, I believe, is to be true, but they can't hold it in or keep it down. Just like Peter Pan in never-never land, you don't want to grow up. But understand that this Christian journey is straight through a battlefield, and some of us are not dressed appropriately to take on our mission: You must put on the full armor of God for the protection that you need.

Ambassadors

We're ambassadors in a foreign country. Soldiers of *the most high* in a war far away from Him trying to make it back home. This world's government is designed to make us fail because they don't fight by our rules. No, the devil cheats. He wants you to think that he's an amateur, but he's a pro. Getting paid with every soul that he can seduce, he and his imps set up roadside bombs and mines that we can't see without our eyes in the sky. That is the reason you have to stay in communication with Headquarters to see what direction or change of direction we must take. Or we could find ourselves behind enemy lines.

But you can't stop fighting now because the only way that we're getting back home is to fight our way back. And in ending this chapter, I want to say to each and every one of you Christian warriors.

We have to remember that as long as we are in this body, the war is not over yet. You must continue to fight. You will have times for R & R, rest and relaxation, but know that your presence is needed on the battlefield. Don't stay gone too long. 'Cause somebody needs you to back them up, speak a word, or send up a prayer. You are a very important member in this army. You are important to me, as the song says, I need you to survive…Your gift is being called forth at the right time, in the right season, for the right position, for a strategic push toward victory. Don't lose sight of your sword, and be sure to keep on the rest of your armor. Sleep in it, eat in it, walk in it, run in it 'cause there is no telling where there may be an ambush coming. Hold tightly to the source, Father, Big Papa.

And my friends, I will meet you on the battlefield with my guns blazing, my sword swinging, and my armor shining 'cause I want most of all to please our Father. Beloved, don't be swayed from doing what is right. And continue to hold up the light.

8

POEMS THAT ARE LIKE STREAMS TO MY SOUL

I'm A Christian Fighting Man
I'm strong in the Lord,
And the power of His might
Stands against the devil,
I wrestle and I fight.
I put on the whole armor. Truth, righteousness,
and peace. With faith in our
Father, whose love will never seize. I have my
salvation, the gospel is where stand.
By His Spirit that is within me, I'm a *Christian Fighting Man*!

SHELL

I've been through war,
I've been through hell.
It was hard to endure within this shell.
That debt we took on when Adam fell,
Separated us from Papa, and made us smell.
Then with a surge of passion He paid the cost,
Of the debt we inherited when we were lost,

And what we became through heartache and shame
Then came to believe on Jesus's name.
Then inside this shell was restored the spirit and
The trust He lost in us when we wouldn't hear it.
How He gave His life for us, His sacrifice. To serve
His Kingdom I won't think twice. And with His Blood
That was shed for the remission of sin, we can rejoin
With Him forever on the last day. Amen.

WRESTLING MATCH

I find myself in a wrestling match. Within a body that is
Wounded, over one eye a patch. Unable to see clearly
It takes control, but I cannot let it sell my soul. Deep
Within I hear the call of God, that beckons me to come
Within this pod, shaking and pulling me to throw a
Powerful blow, and confess my savior to strengthen His
flow. Now the wrestling match is all but won as I fight
I'm empowered by His Son. With the Holy Spirit as my
Cornerman and He as referee I can stand. I place my life
within His hands 'cause He loves me I know, I'm in His
plan. And a champion I'll become 'cause victory is mine
as I choose my Father, I didn't stay blind.

IMMORTAL COMBAT

I was spirit before this age of flesh, I'll be spirit when I leave.
The only thing that shone forth in me
was the time spent in between.
Thou I have constant battles, with enemies
never seen. I have no fear
Of immortal combat, because it's him on which I lean.
The enemy is tricky, slick and specializes
in counterfeit. But he better

67

Watch his step 'cause he don't know who he's messing with.
The power of his name has been giving, and I won't hesitate to call.
Maybe that's what Adam should have done—a long time before the
Fall.
So immortal combat it will be I'm not about to lie down. Or fall or
Bow down to this chump, before I receive my crown.

ABOUT THE AUTHOR

Rev. Lacy Green Jr. was born on May 4, 1957 in St. Eugene Hospital, Dillon, South Carolina. His parents are Lacy Green Sr. and Willina Smutherman Green. Both of Dillon. He attended the schools of the little town until he graduated from Dillon High School in 1975. He worked in a plant called Dixie Anna Mills, a carpet factory for seven years and then joined the United States Army, 82nd Airborne Division, Fort Brag, North Carolina in 1982.

He served in the Gulf War, Desert Shield-Desert Storm and exited the service ETS in September 29, 1992, holding the rank of staff sergeant. Reverend Green is a well-established martial artist holding a rank of 9ᵗʰ degree black belt and has been inducted in three national and international Martial Arts Hall of Fames, one for lifelong achievement, Grand Master of the year, and Fighting Champion of the decade.

He's a man called to preach the Word Of God, and his greatest ministry is to the youthful church. Called as a prophet; he deals with the great prophets of old and strives to speak the true Word of the Most High. He says "I will speak the words of the Prophets of old, for theirs is the word of God."

CPSIA information can be obtained
at www.ICGtesting.com
Printed in the USA
BVHW081600230921
617409BV00003B/289